Railway Memories No. 33

A NORTH WEST PICTURE GALLERY

Compiled by Stephen Chapman

The harsh winter frost maintains its grip on the West Coast main line track as the first of the Duchess Pacifics, No. 46220 *Coronation*, rushes a Carlisle-Euston express past Burton & Holme, north of Carnforth, in early 1963. The line going off to the right went to Holme Mills where there was a factory making cocoa mats - every home had one at the doorstep back in the old days.
Eric Bentley/Stephen Chapman archive

This book is for enjoyment purposes only

BELLCODE BOOKS
Church View, Middle Street
Rudston, East Yorkshire YO25 4UF
email: bellcode4books@yahoo.co.uk

ABOVE: **An early 1950s scene on the through platform at Manchester London Road(Piccadilly since 1960) with an arriving Manchester South Junction & Altrincham 1500 volt dc electric unit, motor brake second No. M28576 leading.** *Tom Greaves*

BELOW: **A northbound freight forges past Ribblehead and approaches the viaduct. Thanks to an optical illusion, the train appears to be going downhill when in fact it is climbing a 1 in 100 gradient.** *Jack Wild/Stephen Chapman archive*

CHESHIRE

ABOVE: The county of Cheshire is home to Crewe - one of the most famous railway centres of all time. In this 1950s scene, Class 4P Compound 4-4-0 No. 40925 of Llandudno Junction is in the station keeping company with a Stanier Class 5 4-6-0. *Stephen Chapman archive*

BELOW: A visitor to Crewe from West Yorkshire on Sunday 5th September 1965 was Low Moor-based Jubilee 4-6-0 No. 45565 *Victoria* with the Halifax Railfans' South Yorkshireman railtour, 1X16 from Bradford Exchange. *Jack Wild/Stephen Chapman archive*

ABOVE: On Crewe North shed is Standard Class 5 4-6-0 No. 73143, a visitor from Rowsley and one of the Caprotti valve gear variants. The date with the negative was 10th November 1953 but as 73143 has the later British Railways crest on its tender and a Type 4 diesel sits in the background this cannot be - 1958 perhaps. The coaling tower and twin ash hoists were prominent landmarks. *Stephen Chapman archive*

BELOW: Crewe South shed, oozing atmosphere on 5th September 1965 with a good selection of active steam locomotives present. Central to the picture is Britannia Pacific No. 70052 *Firth of Tay* with another "Brit" on the left. Between them is a Jubilee 4-6-0 and on the right a pair of 3F "Jinty" 0-6-0 tanks. *Jack Wild/Stephen Chapman archive*

ABOVE: Jubilee No. 45565 *Victoria* **undergoes servicing on Crewe South depot after her arrival with the railtour from Bradford on 5th September 1965.** *Jack Wild/Stephen Chapman archive*

BELOW: Still at Crewe South, the driver of 3F 0-6-0T No. 47450 is conveniently looking the other way as the water tank overflows. No doubt it'll be the fireman's job to get an unwelcome shower while turning off the water column. *Jack Wild/Stephen Chapman archive*

5

ABOVE: A closer view of Britannia No. 70052 *Firth of Tay* on Crewe South shed. *Jack Wild/Stephen Chapman archive*

BELOW: Not just another diesel shunter. This is No. 12000, one of the very earliest examples of the highly successful 350hp 0-6-0 diesel electric breed whose design would lead to the Class 08. She was one of the first batch consisting of a prototype and ten production models built from 1934 by Hawthorn, Leslie of Newcastle in collaboration with English Electric. They went into service with the London Midland & Scottish Railway, the LMS going on to order many more. All but three of the originals were sold to the War Department in 1940, the remainder being retained to become BR Nos. 12000 - 12002, all allocated to Crewe South where 12000 is pictured on Sunday 24th May 1959. *Stephen Chapman archive*

ABOVE: A visit to Crewe Works on Sunday 5th September 1965 found withdrawn BR Standard 8P Pacific No. 71000 *Duke of Gloucester* in open store and awaiting its fate which, as we all know, turned out well in the end. *Jack Wild/Stephen Chapman archive*

BELOW: And a visit to Crewe Works just over 16 years later on 22nd May 1982 found English Electric Type 4 No. 40118 up on jacks and undergoing a major repair. By this time some of her classmates were at the works for scrapping. *Stephen Chapman*

ABOVE: On jacks during maintenance in the slightly more homely works environment of Crewe Diesel Depot on Saturday 22nd May 1982 was English Electric Type 4 No. 40131. *Stephen Chapman*

BELOW: A whole host of railway activities went on at Crewe besides the locomotive works, depots, yards and railway operations. It was also the heart of British Rail's vast stationery supply network operated by the Paper & Printing Dept. Its workload included tickets and this is the ticket printing shop on Friday 10th February 1989. At this time BR had just ceased producing the classic Edmondson card tickets which latterly it was printing only for the heritage railways. *Stephen Chapman*

ABOVE: The Paper & Printing centre on Wistaston Road had its own rail loading bay as seen here on 10th February 1989. Hampers and parcels of stationery were loaded into these vans which were shunted to the station where the contents were transferred to parcels and passenger trains for onward distribution across the whole country. *Stephen Chapman*

BELOW: South of Crewe along the West Coast main line, and in Staffordshire, was the Madeley Chord, a spur laid in the 1960s allowing Silverdale and Holditch collieries, Newcastle-under-Lyme, to be served from the main line following closure of the Stoke-Wellington line. In this November 1992 scene, Brush Type 5 No. 60061 is on the chord with MGR wagons and is approaching the junction with the Silverdale branch (the former Stoke line) near the site of Madeley Road station. *Malcolm Roughley/Stephen Chapman archive*

ABOVE: Chester was - and still is - another important railway junction once served by several railway companies' lines. This undated early 1960s view shows ex-Great Western County class 4-6-0 No. 1027 *County of Stafford* ready to leave Chester General with an express for Shrewsbury and beyond. No details are given but it seems likely to be a Birkenhead-Paddington express. *Stephen Chapman archive*

BELOW: With popular holiday resorts like Prestatyn, Rhyl and Llandudno along the North Wales coast, Chester could be a hectic place on summer Saturdays when many extra trains were run for the multitudes who were starting and ending their summer holidays. In this scene to delight the enthusiast at the west end of Chester General on 4th August 1962, Llandudno Junction's rebuilt Patriot 4-6-0 No. 45534 *E. Tootal Broadhurst* threads its Euston-bound express through the bustling hive of steam activity while pulling into the station. On the left, the engine of a westbound train is taking water while 2-6-4 tanks Nos. 42459 and 42212 stand ready for their next jobs. *Stephen Chapman archive*

ABOVE: Chester and the Wirral were parts where the Great Western penetrated the North West of England in search of the commercial prizes offered by Merseyside. Here, 28xx 2-8-0 No. 3815 of Croes Newydd heads a Wrexham-Birkenhead freight through Bromborough in the late 1950s. *Rev. David Benson*

BELOW: On the line from Chester to Warrington, Class 5 4-6-0 No. 44712 blasts a 1960s northbound class 4 fully fitted express freight through Frodsham. Of additional interest are the old tenders in the goods yard. *Peter Reeves/Stephen Chapman archive*

ABOVE: At the southern end of the Warrington railway complex a 9F 2-10-0, unidentified due to having lost its number plate, thrashes over the River Mersey bridge at Walton New Junction with an Up West Coast main line freight in the mid-1960s. *Arthur Chester*

BELOW: At Walton Old Junction, on what was the main line before the Manchester Ship Canal was built requiring a higher level line and a new bridge, smartly turned out Stanier Class 5 4-6-0 No. 45130 of Croes Newydd shed passes sister No. 45158 while working a freight bound for North Wales. Heavy freights climbing up to the "new" West Coast main line at Acton Grange Junction might require rear-end assistance and the exhaust of the banking engine can just be seen at the far end of the train. *Arthur Chester*

ABOVE: Destined to become the last British Rail standard gauge steam locomotive to run under its own steam, Britannia Pacific No. 70013 *Oliver Cromwell* awaits departure from Walton Old Junction with a 1960s night freight to its Carlisle home. *Arthur Chester*

BELOW: Still at Walton Old Junction, a water spout from a disconnected hydrant brings an ornamental touch to this view of English Electric 350hp 0-6-0 diesel shunter No. 12076, one of the immediate successors to 12000 on page 6. Introduced in 1945 these examples would become BR class 11. It would appear that 12076 had just had its radiator topped up. *Arthur Chester*

ABOVE: At Warrington's Dallam shed, the raw power of steam is epitomized by this trio fired up and ready for work. Nearest is 8F 2-8-0 No. 48681 and in the centre is Stanier Class 5 - a class more often referred to as "Black Five" - 4-6-0 No. 44892. *Arthur Chester*

BELOW: One of Sutton Oak shed's BR Standard Class 4 2-6-0s, No. 76078, heads a 1960s trip freight, probably bound for St. Helens, along the West Coast main line at Winwick Quay, north of Warrington. *Arthur Chester*

ABOVE: An early 1960s scene in which un-named Patriot 4-6-0 No. 45550 awaits departure from Winwick Quay sidings with an Up fully braked Class 4 freight. *Arthur Chester*

BELOW: Royal Scot 4-6-0 No. 46115 *Scots Guardsman* - one of two members of its class to be preserved - is held by signals at Winwick Quay while travelling northbound tender-first. *Arthur Chester*

ABOVE: Having just passed Winwick Junction, the Glasgow to Euston Royal Scot is headed by English Electric Type 4 No. D342. On the skyline can be seen Vulcan Foundry where lettering on the roof reads: "Vulcan Locomotives." *Arthur Chester*

BELOW: On the Cheshire Lines Committee route between Manchester and Liverpool, Ivatt Class 4 2-6-0 No. 43040 passes Glazebrook station with a westbound train of empty coaching stock. On the right is the small station goods yard with its 5-ton crane. Despite its modest size it was listed in the Railway Clearing House Handbook of Stations as able to handle all classes of freight. It closed to goods in August 1964. East of the station, beyond the overbridge, were the extensive Glazebrook Exchange sidings which gave access to the Manchester Ship Canal Railway, coal staiths on the canal, Irlam steel works and other large factories as well as a line passing over the canal to Skelton Junction on the Warrington-Stockport line. *Peter Reeves/Stephen Chapman archive*

ABOVE: The Great Central "Director" 4-4-0s of LNER Class D10 were a principal form of motive power for passenger trains on the Cheshire Lines Committee routes. This is LNER No. 2652 *Edwin A. Beazley* on Northwich shed in the late 1940s, shortly before nationalisation, after which it would become BR No. 62652. *Stephen Chapman archive*

BELOW: At Altrincham, the Cheshire Lines route from Chester via Northwich rubbed shoulders with the Manchester South Junction & Altrincham suburban route to Manchester which was electrified at 1500 volts dc. The 3-car MSJ&A units were kept at Altrincham car sheds, just west of the station. Examples of the 1930s-built sets are seen there from a passing train in the 1950s with motor brake second No. M28578 the nearest. *Tom Greaves*

ABOVE: By now, the Class 304 ac units that replaced the dc sets on the MSJ&A line have become vintage classics, having themselves disappeared into history. Here, set No. 304007 is framed by the glorious ironwork of Altrincham station in 1991 while awaiting departure. In dc days, the line extended beyond the back of the train to the car sheds. Not long after this picture the MSJ&A was converted into part of the Manchester Metrolink tram system - when again it became dc. *Stephen Chapman*

BELOW: It's Wednesday 10th May 1967 and the two lads watching "Black Five" No. 44895 shunting Northenden cement terminal will have little more than a year left to appreciate real BR steam at work. *Peter Reeves/Stephen Chapman archive*

RIGHT: Real working steam may have been wonderful to watch but it was downright hard filthy labour for those who had to keep it running. No more so than in a manual coaling stage, such as here at Heaton Mersey shed.
Rev. David Benson

BELOW: Just south of Stockport, London & North Western "Cauliflower" 2F 0-6-0 No. 58426 is seen at Adswood with a short empty wagon train on a dull Monday 31st July 1950.
Stephen Chapman archive

ABOVE: Stockport Edgeley shed visit in 1948. Engines on view and still bearing LMS alongside their new BR numbers, are Stanier 2-6-4T No. 42463, a 3F 0-6-0T and ex-London & North Western G1(Class 6F) 0-8-0 No. 49098. *Tom Greaves*

BELOW: Stanier 2-6-4T No. 42664 gathers pace with a Cheshire Lines route Manchester London Road to Liverpool class A service as it passes the Manchester United football stadium at Trafford Park Junction in the early 1950s. *Tom Greaves*

GREATER MANCHESTER

On the island platform at Manchester London Road, today's Manchester Piccadilly platforms 13 and 14, in the early 1950s, we are given a view of both ends of a MSJ&A line electric unit. Above, is motor brake second No. M28576 with foot holds and handrails for access to the electrical gear on the roof - hopefully when the "juice" is off. The enamel Virol advertisement is one of the enduring symbols of the age. Below, driving trailer second No. M29241 has a much plainer look, requiring no foot holds and hand rails. The centre cars, incidentally, were also trailers and included first class accommodation. *Tom Greaves*

ABOVE: This view on a wintry Sunday 17th December 1961 shows an MSJ&A unit at Stretford with motor brake second No. M28575M leading. *Stephen Chapman archive*

BELOW: Now a vintage dc electric locomotive. Class 76 EM1 Bo-Bo No. E26056 *Triton* starts out from Manchester Piccadilly with an express to Sheffield via Woodhead formed of newly reliveried blue and grey stock on Saturday 3rd May 1969. In less than a year this passenger service would be withdrawn but the Class 76s would continue to haul freight over the Woodhead line until its closure in 1981. *Stephen Chapman archive*

Piccadilly, Victoria, Exchange, Central, Oxford Road. There was one more - and this is Manchester's forgotten station. Manchester Mayfield was a terminus dedicated to suburban services. It was situated next to Piccadilly and connected to the Piccadilly approach lines via a bridge over Temperance Street. It closed on 28th August 1960, was converted to a parcels depot in 1970 but closed finally as BR progressively opted out of the parcels business. Above, a Class 08 shunts vans at Mayfield in 1985. Below: The Mayfield interior, also in 1985. A diesel parcels unit can just be seen on the left. *Malcolm Roughley/Stephen Chapman archive*

BELOW: Over at Manchester Central, D10 "Director" 4-4-0 No. 62654 *Walter Burgh Gair* arrives with an express on Wednesday 25th April 1951. *Stephen Chapman archive*

ABOVE: At Manchester Central, ex-Great Central Robinson-designed Class B9 4-6-0 No. 1475 rests by the turntable on Thursday 24th April 1947. When withdrawn from service three years later its number was taken by one of the North Eastern B16 4-6-0s which were renumbered to make way for the final build of B1 4-6-0s. Manchester Central was closed in May 1969 but the impressive arched trainshed, designed to mirror St. Pancras, survives as the G-Mex exhibition centre. *Stephen Chapman archive*

BELOW: The east Manchester district of Gorton was the most important place of all on the Great Central network, at least so far as motive power was concerned. Here were the main loco works, a wagon works and a principal motive power depot, coded 39A by British Railways in the 1950s. With the wagon works over the wall in the background, D10 4-4-0 No. 62659 *Worsley-Taylor* simmers on the depot in the early 1950s alongside Class N5 0-6-2T No. 69326. *Tom Greaves*

ABOVE: Going out of Manchester along the Great Central line comes the important and interesting junction of Guide Bridge. Class C14 4-4-2T No. 67450 calls there with a Manchester-Glossop service in May 1952. *Peter Cookson collection*

BELOW: When Guide Bridge was ceasing to be a place of interest, at least for the enthusiast. It is Saturday 8th May 1982, the Woodhead line to Sheffield has been closed east of Hadfield and the redundant Class 76 dc electric locos are lined up awaiting their fate. The nearest pair are 76028 and 76032. *Stephen Chapman*

ABOVE: An early 1950s view from the platform at Manchester Exchange station as Patricroft shed's G2a class 7F 0-8-0 No. 49335 heads past on an eastbound local trip freight. No. 49335 was one of the numerous batch of ex-LNWR G1 class rebuilt from 1936 onwards with 175lb per sq. in. G2 Belpaire boilers.
Tom Greaves

LEFT: The view from a "Peak" - hauled Newcastle-Liverpool train pulling out of Manchester Exchange in March 1968. This former LNWR station was closed on 5th May 1969 and its services switched to the neighbouring former Lancashire & Yorkshire Victoria station.
Stephen Chapman

ABOVE: Awaiting departure at the west end of Manchester Exchange in the 1960s is Crewe North Jubilee 4-6-0 No. 45554 *Ontario*. With only the one headlamp over the left buffer so far it is impossible to assess what kind of train she is about to work, whether express passenger, parcels or empty coaching stock; one parcels van can be seen behind the engine. *Arthur Chester*

BELOW: The classic steam era Manchester Victoria scene - and one which continued well into the diesel era. On Saturday 18th June 1955 ex-Lancashire & Yorkshire Aspinall 3F 0-6-0 No. 52159 is standing by to provide rear end banking assistance to any train that should need it on the 1 in 59/47 climb to Miles Platting. *David Holmes*

ABOVE: **London & North Western line trains on the Trans-Pennine route used Exchange station and passed through Victoria station on the centre roads until the closure of Exchange in 1969. Patriot 4-6-0 No. 45537** *Private E. Sykes V.C.* **looks to be taking a run at Miles Platting bank as it storms through Victoria with an eastbound express on Friday 24th August 1951.** *Stephen Chapman archive*

BELOW: **The Great Central J11 class 0-6-0s were more likely to be found on the south side of Manchester but No. 64420 of Gorton was on railtour duty with the Railway Correspondence & Travel Society special of Saturday 23rd September 1961.** *Arthur Wilson*

ABOVE: Until the total rebuilding of the through platforms in the 1990s, Manchester Victoria retained a real steam age atmosphere even though steam was long gone. Here, English Electric Type 4 No. 40106 - the last BR member of the class to wear steam-era green livery - has arrived with the 11.16 from Bangor on Saturday 28th August 1982. *Stephen Chapman*

BELOW: In the above picture 40106 was in her orginal BR green but Brush Type 4 No. D1842 and Hymek No. D7076(a product of the Beyer Peacock works in Gorton) have been restored back to green livery. They were in the loco siding awaiting movement back home after attending a diesel gala at the East Lancashire Railway. It is 1990 and the Class 31 is on the Warrington-Heywood trip. *Stephen Chapman*

ABOVE: In August 1984 Wilsons Brewery in Manchester celebrated its 150th anniversary with a special steam working for invited guests from Manchester Victoria to a temporary platform erected alongside the brewery - at Brewery Sidings no less - just beyond Miles Platting. Preserved LNWR 0-6-2 "Coal Tank" No. 1054 is pictured with one of the runs from Manchester Victoria as it passes over the slow line that still ran behind Miles Platting station at that time. *Stephen Chapman*

BELOW: Newton Heath was the biggest motive power depot on the L&Y system and today it is just as important, providing diesel multiple units for services all over the North West. The atmosphere was very different in steam days however, as pictured here. On what looks like a typical British summer's day in August 1963, Britannia Pacific No. 70051 *Firth of Forth* is in unglamorous surroundings while on the pits and making its way towards the coal plant. *Jack Wild/Stephen Chapman archive*

ABOVE: Still at Newton Heath on the same day as the previous picture, 9F 2-10-0 No. 92161 has come on shed after working a special parcels train, or a high priority special freight such as a fish train. *Jack Wild/Stephen Chapman archive*

BELOW: Nowadays, trains between Manchester and Rochdale on the former Lancashire & Yorkshire main line fly past the site of Middleton Junction as if it never existed. Nothing remains but as can be seen, it was once a fairly significant railway location. In this 1950s scene, ex-Lancashire & Yorkshire 2-4-2T No. 50777 pulls out of the station past Middleton Junction East signal box with a Rochdale-bound train. In the foreground is the branch to Middleton itself while the coaches in the background are on the branch to Oldham Werneth via Chadderton. The leaning mill chimney can be accredited to distortion by the camera lens - let's hope!
Stephen Chapman archive

ABOVE: The branch terminus at Middleton looked to be in a pretty desperate state when this Derby Works 2-car DMU was arriving from Manchester Victoria in March 1964. The total neglect was a symptom of impending closure which took place with effect from 7th September. Goods facilities were withdrawn just over a year later, on 11th October 1965. *Jack Wild/Stephen Chapman archive*

BELOW: Oldham Werneth where in the 1950s Stanier 2-6-4T No. 42618 works hard while bringing a stopping passenger train from Manchester Victoria off the Chadderton branch from Middleton Junction - part of which had a gradient as steep as 1 in 27. Werneth station and the line on the left survived the closure of the Chadderton branch but recent years have seen the Oldham Loop converted to the Metrolink tram system and the line now deviates to the right to run along the streets of Oldham before resuming its original path to Rochdale. *Stephen Chapman archive*

ABOVE: Oldham once had five stations. After Werneth, through two tunnels, came Central which adjoined Clegg Street station on the Oldham, Ashton & Guide Bridge Railway coming in from Ashton Oldham Road to form a "V" shape station. This March 1964 view approaching from Ashton is of Clegg Street. With Mumps station only a short distance further along the line, Central closed in April 1966 while Clegg Street had closed in May 1959, though a major parcels depot connected with catalogue shopping was in operation there until the 1980s. *Both pictures on this page: Jack Wild/Stephen Chapman archive*

BELOW: Another short milltown branch that was doomed not to survive the Beeching era was that to Royton, from Royton Junction just west of Oldham on the Rochdale line. A Derby Works DMU is seen there in March 1964. Royton also closed to passengers in April 1966, while the goods and coal yards, far more extensive than the modest station, had closed in November 1964.

ABOVE: North West England can still be seen to have a relatively substantial railway network but a look at any 1950s map reveals a mesmerizing conglomeration of lines striving to reach every mill town and colliery - anywhere where there was business to be had and money to be made, more usually from goods and coal rather than passengers. One such line was the Facit branch from Rochdale to Bacup, part of which survived until August 1967 to serve the goods yard at Whitworth and a private siding at Shawclough & Healey. On Sunday 19th February, brake van tours were run on the line using preserved L&Y "Pug" 0-4-0ST No. 51218, this one for the Roche Valley Railway Society is seen at Shawclough. *This picture: Stephen Chapman archive. Below: Stephen Chapman*

BELOW: In modern times Castleton still had much to delight the observer, as pictured here on 17th May 1989. A Stanlow-Jarrow fuel train hauled by Class 47 No. 47119 is held in the loop at Castleton East Junction after releasing the assisting engine which had piloted it from Warrington to help with the continuous gradient from Manchester Victoria. On the right are the now closed rail welding depot and the branch to Heywood which has since been reinstated through to Bury as a heritage line by the East Lancashire Railway.

ABOVE: On the Castleton-Bury line, a WD 2-8-0 heads a Yorkshire-bound train of empty wagons through Heywood in the 1960s. The odd mixture of wagons in the sidings on the right are a clue to the presence of a wagon works situated behind the photographer. Later, under the ownership of the Standard Wagon Co., the works kept this section of the line open long to become part of today's East Lancashire Railway. It is here we can reflect on the motivational names Victorian millowners often bestowed on their premises for the one on the right was called the Perseverance Mill. *Both pictures: Stephen Chapman archive*

BELOW: Caprotti valve gear equipped BR Standard Class 5 No. 73139 of Rowsley shed was well away from home when caught leaving Bury Knowsley Street on 28th July 1962 with train 1J01, the 8.50am Liverpool Exchange-Rochdale. it was extended to Scarborough Londesborough Road on summer Saturdays, as was the case here.

ABOVE: When the Class EM2 Co-Co electric locos used for express passenger services on the Manchester-Sheffield Woodhead line were taken out of service in March 1968 they were placed in store at Bury shed before being officially withdrawn that October. Considered worthy of better than scrap, they were later sold to the Netherlands for a new lease of life. On Saturday 25th May 1968, Nos. E27001 *Ariadne* and E27006 *Pandora* were among those present in Bury's Buckley Wells shed. *Stephen Chapman archive*

BELOW: On the Bury-Tottington branch, ex-L&Y 0-6-0 No. 52523 brings up the rear on a Roche Valley Railway Society railtour near Woolfold on Saturday 28th July 1962. Heading the train at this point was Fowler Class 3 2-6-2T No. 40063 which had been brought out of store from Bolton shed for the occasion. *Stephen Chapman archive*

ABOVE: The terminus of the Tottington branch was Holcombe Brook until May 1960 after which it went only as far as Tottington which itself closed completely in August 1963. The branch passenger service, which at one time had been electric as an extension of the Bury-Manchester service, was withdrawn from 5th May 1952. On Tuesday 24th April 1951, the crew of L&Y Radial tank No. 50829 take a break on the platform seat at Holcombe Brook following arrival from Bury. *H. C. Casserley/Stephen Chapman archive*

BELOW: A service hanging on by a thread to this day is that between Stockport and Stalybridge which once provided a useful connection for passengers travelling between West Yorkshire and such places as Crewe, Stoke, and Wolverhampton. Although it serves intermediate stations, it became largely redundant when Trans-Pennine services were switched from Manchester Victoria to Piccadilly. At the time of writing, the service consists of just one train(sometimes a bus) each way a week, on Saturdays, maintained in order to avoid the bother of going through the official closure procedure when the route itself is still required for freight. This 1982 scene shows a Gloucester Railway Carriage & Wagon Class 100 DMU arriving at Stalybridge with a service from Stockport. *Stephen Chapman*

ABOVE: Another of the short branches serving mill towns was that between Saddleworth Junction and Delph whose passenger service was affectionately known as the "Delph Donkey." In this 1950s view, Ivatt Class 2 2-6-2T No. 41282 of Lees shed, Oldham, hugs the hillside near Measurements Halt with the "Donkey" to Delph. The service was withdrawn from 2nd May 1955 while goods traffic lasted until November 1963. *Stephen Chapman archive*

BELOW: In this April 1954 view it is Fowler Class 3 2-6-2T No. 40057 doing the honours with the "Donkey," this time near Dobcross. *Peter Cookson Collection*

ABOVE: At Diggle, the main Trans-Pennine route divided into two, the line that is still used today passing through Greenfield and Mossley, and the other through Upper Mill, Friezland, Roaches and Micklehurst before they reunited at Stalybridge. The Micklehurst line lost its local passenger service as long ago as 1917 and goods services were withdrawn in the mid-1960s. It closed completely in late 1966 but for the Stalybridge end which was kept to serve Hartshead power station where steam, in the form of a Hawthorn Leslie fireless locomotive and a Robert Stephenson & Hawthorns 0-4-0ST, worked on into the 1970s. On 2nd October 1966, the line was traversed by the Stephenson Locomotive Society's Pennine Rail Tour, seen passing Friezland signal box behind Britannia No. 70004 *William Shakespeare* which worked the train from Stockport to Leeds. Until 1974, this area including Delph and right up to the edge of Oldham was in Yorkshire, the county boundary actually running through the shed yard at Lees. *Neville Stead colln./Transport Library*

BELOW: This odd working seen at Diggle on Saturday 12th June 1982, hauled by Class 25 No. 25034, is the "paraffin special" from Manchester which delivered stores to various outlying signal boxes. *Stephen Chapman*

ABOVE: Workworn BR Standard Class 5 4-6-0 No. 73034 was making for her home depot at Patricroft when overtaken by a Newcastle-Liverpool train on Salford viaducts in March 1968. Lower down on the left is the site of Salford goods yard. The leaning spire is not an attempt to out-do Chesterfield but distortion from the lens of a Kodak Brownie 44A camera.
Stephen Chapman

LEFT: Ex-LMS Fowler 2F 0-6-0 tank No. 47165 blasts out from under the Liverpool line and into Salford goods yard while taking a run at the Salford incline up to the main line after shunting Irwell Street sidings on September 15th 1962. Introduced in 1928, these mini-Jinties were designed with a short wheelbase especially for shunting in confined areas often beset with sharp curves, such as docks and goods stations.
Robert Anderson

The following six pictures feature the Mode Wheel Railtour of Salford Docks, a brakevan special run by the Roch Valley Railway Society and Locomotive Club of Great Britain on 29th October 1967, again with preserved L&Y "Pug" No. 51218 as the motive power. No details as to the precise locations came with these negatives so a good deal of research with Ordnance Survey maps and other sources has been necessary but the results should not be taken as gospel. ABOVE: Judging by the relative position of Barton power station chimneys the special is alongside Taylor Road on the Trafford Park Railway, on a branch which led to a large textile machinery works.

BELOW: This looks to be on the swing bridge over the Bridgewater Canal carrying the connection from Westinghouse Road, on Trafford Park Estate, to Trafford Park BR sidings. *Both Stephen Chapman archive*

ABOVE: No doubts about this spot. A fine array of Manchester Ship Canal Railway Hudswell Clarke 0-6-0 tanks on shed at the legendary Mode Wheel depot. The pair standing out front are Nos. 35(left) and 50.

BELOW: Hudswell Clarke 0-6-0T No. 67 was used on the MSC Railway section of the tour and is seen here on Sunday 29th October 1967 causing a moment of concern on the points at what appears to be Trafford Wharf Road sidings. *Both Stephen Chapman archive*

ABOVE: Some elderly MSC Railway wagons on the left form the background to this spot with No. 67 among the bushes.

BELOW: This shot with 67 and 51218 double heading appears to be looking east in the once extensive sidings at Trafford Wharf Road.
Both Stephen Chapman archive

ABOVE: Back at Mode Wheel, Hudswell Clarke 0-6-0T No. 35 is on this occasion nicely bulled up and in steam. *Stephen Chapman Archive*

BELOW: In the 1970s the MSC Railway - and its Trafford Park Estate counterpart - went into a steady decline alongside the terminal decline of the docks until the MSC Railway was ultimately reduced to just isolated sections at Weaste, Ellesmere Port, Stanlow, and Barton Dock where a new loco shed was built for engines working main line trains alongside Barton Dock Road to and from the new Containerbase. But the main works and loco shed at Mode Wheel carried on and this January 1986 view inside the works shows Sentinel 4-wheel diesel hydraulic No. DH23(builders' No. 10226 of 1965) undergoing repairs. *Malcolm Roughley/Stephen Chapman Archive*

ABOVE: On the same day, another pair of 1965-built Sentinel 4-wheel diesel hydraulics were being refuelled. They are No. DH24 (10227) and DH26(10229.) *Malcolm Roughley/Stephen Chapman Archive*

BELOW: When the MSC Railway first began ordering diesels they remained largely loyal to their Leeds-based builder. This pair at Mode Wheel in January 1986, Nos. D3 and D11 are Hudswell Clarke 0-6-0 diesel mechanical locos D1188, built 1960 and D1255, built 1962. *Malcolm Roughley/Stephen Chapman Archive*

ABOVE: By the time of this January 1986 view, just about the only remaining task for the MSCR's Mode Wheel fleet was to shunt tank wagons brought in by British Rail. In this view from the cab of one of the Sentinel locos at Weaste, a BR Class 47 is seen on the main line connection which came from the Liverpool & Manchester line at Eccles. It can be seen, especially on the left, that most of this railway complex had been abandoned and Mode Wheel itself would soon go. A rail-served cement terminal operated purely by main line locos was opened on the site in July 2000. Sadly, all vestige of this once great system and the Trafford Park Railway is gone. But at least the Metrolink trams now run nearby and are well worth exploring. *Malcolm Roughley/Stephen Chapman Archive*

BELOW: Back to steam days. At Eccles Junction in the 1950s, un-named Patriot 4-6-0 No. 45542 leaves the Liverpool & Manchester line with an express and joins the route that will take it to the right of Patricroft engine shed and onward to Liverpool via Tyldsley and Leigh. *Stephen Chapman Archive*

ABOVE: **No. 47165 now at rest on Agecroft shed in October 1961.** *Stephen Chapman Archive*

BELOW: **Besides the Manchester Ship Canal and Trafford Park railways, a whole network of colliery lines operated by the National Coal Board was superimposed on the tangle of railways making up the main line system in what was then Lancashire. One of the most extensive was the Walkden Collieries system which was noted for its ex-North Staffordshire Railway 0-6-2 tanks. One of those was** *Princess*, **seen shunting four BR wagons over the Eccles-Bolton Great Moor Street line at Walkden in 1951.** *Stephen Chapman Archive*

ABOVE: Further up the Great Moor Street line was Little Hulton, junction with a mineral branch to Brackley Colliery and the Walkden system. It seemed to be open house on the Brackley Colliery branch on Saturday 21st September 1963 when the Great Moor Street - Little Hulton leg of the LCGB's South Lancashire Limited railtour was turning back there. "Jinty" 3F 0-6-0T No. 47378 had brought the train from Bolton and is seen ready to return after running round. The overbridge in the left background carries a lane over the Eccles-Bolton line. *Jack Wild/Stephen Chapman archive*

BELOW: A little further along the main line - for this was the LNWR's own main line to Bolton - we reach Plodder Lane where the motive power depot was situated along with a goods depot. On Saturday 28th June 1958, with the loco yard on the left and the goods yard on the right, a "Black Five" 4-6-0 passes with the 1pm Great Moor Street to Llandudno, in its reportedly last year of operation from the Bolton station which had lost its regular passenger services in March 1954. *Stephen Chapman archive*

ABOVE: Now just outside Bolton Great Moor Street on 21st September 1963, Patricroft 8F 2-8-0 No. 48178 is seen alongside the coal yard on the right, in an area known as Lecturers Closes, following arrival from Manchester Liverpool Road with the LCGB South Lancashire Limited railtour. The special was then taken to Little Hulton by 0-6-0T No. 47378 which required banking assistance from the 8F after stalling on a gradient. *Jack Wild/Stephen Chapman archive*

BELOW: Now at the L&Y side of Bolton with pristine Aspinal 3F 0-6-0 No. 12528 neatly posed on shed in the 1930s. *Arthur Wilson*

ABOVE: Steam activity at Bolton Trinity Street. On Wednesday 10th June 1959 WD 2-8-0 No. 90204 plods through the station with a local goods while Patriot 4-6-0 No. 45509 *The Derbyshire Yeomanry* passes in the Manchester direction. *Stephen Chapman archive*

BELOW: In a scene packed with railway interest, another WD, No. 90121, waits near the junction with the Bury line. Behind it is the Manchester Road goods yard with its huge warehouse on the left and travelling crane behind the signals on the right.
Peter Reeves/Stephen Chapman archive

ABOVE: If the railway authorities think they have a problem with trespass when a steam special runs nowadays, this would give them nightmares for weeks. No doubt all signals would have to be thrown to danger and all trains stopped as enthusiasts besieged the track and climbed the signals at Bolton Trinity Street on 28th July 1968. One lad in the centre is even skipping or running across the points. At least it was a Sunday. The object of their devil-may-care attention was 8F 2-8-0 No. 48773 on a farewell to steam railtour.

BELOW: In a more sober scene on Tuesday 24th April 1951, ex-L&Y 2F 0-6-0ST No. 51513 shunts Manchester Road goods yard while overlooked by the 40-ton travelling crane. *Both Stephen Chapman archive*

ABOVE: An especially pleasing feature at certain ex-L&Y stations were these model Isle of Man Steam Packet ships displayed to encourage travel there by train and ferry. This one, still at Bolton on 10th January 1987, is *King Orry*. *Stephen Chapman*

BELOW: Steam has been gone 14 years but there was still plenty of interest at Bolton on Saturday 28th August 1982 when Class 47 No. 47485 was caught departing on the 07.55 Barrow-Manchester Victoria. Manchester Road goods yard was still in business at this time, semaphore signals still ruled and the huge overline station buildings still cast a shadow over the platforms below. *Stephen Chapman*

ABOVE: By the time of this view on Wednesday 24th August 1988 much had changed at Bolton. The signalling had been modernized and brought under the control of Manchester Piccadilly, the goods station had gone, the huge station buildings were demolished and replaced in 1987, the track further rationalized, and the Orlando Street overbridge given a fancy repaint. But there had been some revival in that Bolton had been made a mail terminal. Here we see Class 47 No. 47530 making up a postal train while 47619 arrives with the 18.20 Manchester Victoria-Glasgow. This is the same spot as the picture at the bottom of page 50. *Stephen Chapman*

BELOW: As late as the early 1980s a train journey from Manchester to Bolton would provide views of Robert Stephenson & Hawthorns-built steam saddle tanks at Agecroft power station followed vintage electric locomotives from the same builder at Kearsley power station. At Kearsley the Bo-Bo electric locos were used to haul coal via a short, steeply graded branch between exchange sidings alongside the main line and the power station. This view shows builders' Nos. 7078 of 1944 and 7284 of 1945 on Friday 8th September 1978. By this time the branch was no longer in use with coal delivered by lorry but the locos were still used for internal movements.
Adrian Booth

In the 1960s Horwich works was known for its use of the last surviving ex-L&Y 2F 0-6-0STs which retained their LMS numbers. Seen on 21st September 1963 are:
TOP: No. 11519 in the works loco shed and still in full LMS livery.
CENTRE: No. 11368, sporting the early BR crest, found to be at work.

BOTTOM: The branch terminus at Horwich when visited by the LCGB railtour of 21st September 1963. The 8F, No. 48178 had brought the train in and, after the participants had toured the loco works, 4F 0-6-0 No. 44501 was waiting to take it back to Manchester Central via more fascinating detours. The public passenger service was withdrawn from Horwich in September 1965 and the goods facilities on the left, which were listed as having a 7-ton crane capacity and able to handle all classes of freight, in April 1966, but the branch continued to serve the works for another 20 years. *All Jack Wild/S. Chapman archive*

ABOVE: Horwich, along with Crewe, was also renowned for its internal narrow gauge system operated by diminutive saddle tanks. This is *Wrenn*, pictured on Sunday 3rd February 1957. *Arthur Wilson*

BELOW: BR Standard Class 4 4-6-0 No. 75057 makes a rousing start from the former Great Central station at Hindley South with a 1960s Wigan Central - Manchester Central service running via Lowton St. Mary's and Glazebrook. The signals are evidence of the three-way junction just beyond the bridge. The line on the right went via De Trafford Junction to Whelley Junction where it divided again with lines going to Standish Junction on the West Coast main line north of Wigan, and to Adlington on the Bolton-Preston line. The centre line went to Wigan Central where it terminated, while a line to the left line went to the West Coast main line at Bamfurlong Junction and the Wigan-St. Helens line at Ince Moss Junction. Passenger services were withdrawn in November 1964 and Hindley South closed. The picture is undated but might be on the last day, given that enthusiasts on the train are photographing the photographer.
Stephen Chapman archive

ABOVE: The 21st September 1963 South Lancashire Limited railtour again, this time with 48178 at Wigan Central, the Great Central Railway's terminus. The 8F had brought the tour from Bolton Great Moor Street via Atherton Bag Lane, Chowbent West Junction, Bickershaw Junctions and Hindley South. It is seen here waiting to depart for Horwich via Hindley South, Bickershaw Colliery, Plank Lane, Kenyon Junction, Bamfurlong Sidings, De Trafford Junction and Adlington. *Jack Wild/Stephen Chapman archive*

BELOW: Over on the L&Y side at Wigan Wallgate shed, Fairburn Class 4 2-6-4T No. 42299 is seen by the coaling stage with an ex-L&Y 0-6-0 on Tuesday 14th April 1953. *H.C. Casserley/Stephen Chapman archive*

ABOVE: Oh happy days, summers when the sun always seemed to shine - at least that's how we remember them - a station platform and a constant parade of steam trains. This was Saturday 16th September 1961 over at Wigan North Western where the 10.15am Glasgow-Euston, which was booked to run non-stop from Carlisle to Crewe, was forced to stop for water. Watched by the assembled throng of spotters, the fireman of Class 8P Pacific No. 46246 *City of Manchester* perches on top of the tender while filling up from the water column alongside. *Robert Anderson*

BELOW: Saturday 23rd April 1966, A2 Pacific No. 60528 *Tudor Minstrel* restarts the Altrincham Railway Excursion Society's Waverley Special to Edinburgh via Carlisle and the Waverley line. The train had started from Manchester Exchange at 08.45 and returned via York. The A2 worked as far as Edinburgh, the special returning behind V2 2-6-2s 60836 and 60824, and from York behind Jubilee No. 45565 *Victoria*. *Eric Bentley/Stephen Chapman archive*. With due acknowledgement to the Six Bells Junction website for some of the railtour information in this book.

MERSEYSIDE

ABOVE: Being a great port Liverpool had many fascinating railways, one of the most notable being its innovative overhead railway, known as the "Dockers' Umbrella" since standing underneath gave shelter from the rain. This view of northbound set No. 26 on 22nd May 1956 is at James Street station. The line followed the waterfront passing all the docks for 6½ miles from Seaforth in the north where there were car sheds and a junction with the L&Y North Mersey Line, to Dingle in the south where it ended with a half-mile tunnel. Completed in 1896 it was the world's first overhead electric railway and the first in Britain to use automatic signalling - with electrically operated semaphores. These were replaced in 1921 with Westinghouse colour lights, again the first in this country. Sadly, it had to close at the end of 1956, not through lack of use but because no-one was prepared to fund the £2 million cost of renewing the decking.

BELOW: New Brighton(former Wirral Railway) on 2nd June 1952 with one of the American-style Mersey Railway electric units supplied by Westinghouse when that system was electrified in the early 20th century. This is BR No. M28412. *Both S. Chapman archive*

ABOVE: Where freight and commuters mix. One of the 1930s ex-LMS Wirral line units(later Class 503) on a Liverpool-West Kirby service calls at Bidston station during the late 1950s while 3F 0-6-0T No. 47628 heads a trip working into Bidston sidings.

BELOW: A particularly memorable sight on the Wirral was the iron ore trains that ran from Bidston Dock to the John Summers works at Shotton. Class 9F 2-10-0 No. 92046 is seen with a loaded ore train shortly after passing Bidston Dee Junction in the late 1950s.
Both Rev. David Benson

ABOVE: Birkenhead Docks had an extensive entanglement of railways under the aegis of the Mersey Docks & Harbour Board which were still active and easily explorable well into the 1980s. With the cranes of Cavendish Wharf forming a backdrop, BR 204hp shunter No. 03073 is parked at the junction of Corporation Road and Duke Street during a break in operations on 26th February 1988. Going to the left were Cavendish sidings which by this time were mostly abandoned and containing only a few derelict wagons. *Stephen Chapman*

BELOW: Then as now, Birkenhead's passenger services were mainly part of the Liverpool suburban network but until Bonfire Night 1967 it had a true main line terminus, courtesy of the Great Western/LNWR Birkenhead Joint Railway which provided an outlet to Chester. That was Woodside station where Stanier Class 4 2-6-4T No. 42616 is pictured in around 1966. Previously at Watford, well-travelled 42616 ended her days in October 1967 at Low Moor shed, West Yorkshire, after a spell working the Bradford portions of London expresses. Given her profile and longevity, it is surprising that she was not preserved as a working two-cylinder representative of this class - but she has at least been immortalized by a commercial 00 gauge model. *Stephen Chapman archive*

ABOVE: A reminder of the days when trains ran right down to the Liverpool waterfront with passengers for the Atlantic liners and the ferries. The "Super D" 0-8-0 - hauled train in this 6th June 1959 scene at Liverpool's Riverside station is only carrying gricers, however. Situated between Princes Dock and the floating Princes landing stage, the station belonged to the Mersey Docks & Harbour Board and was served by the LNWR and its successors via the Edge Hill-Bootle line which remains in use today. The station was closed from 1st March 1971, a victim of the jet age along with the liners it served. *R. M. Casserley/Stephen Chapman archive*

BELOW: The Mersey Docks & Harbour Board's railway in Liverpool extended to over 60 miles of lines following the waterfront and reaching into the many docks. It had its own locomotives for shunting and these required engine sheds to be located at strategic points along the way. This one, nestling beneath the Overhead Railway, is believed to be at Huskisson Branch Dock No. 1 alongside Regent Road in the 1950s. The engine facing is Avonside 0-6-0ST No. 14. During the 1960s the docks went into serious decline and by 1973 the railway was as good as out of use. Since the 1980s, however, there has been quite a revival at the northern end between Alexandra Dock and Seaforth but all traffic is now worked by main line locos. *Stephen Chapman archive*

ABOVE: The grace and magnificence of Lime Street station's great arched roof and of the Coronation class Pacifics that took its expresses to Euston. Here, on Sunday 20th September 1959, parcels are loaded aboard a London express headed by No. 46231 *Duchess of Atholl* - the subject of a Liverpool-made Hornby Dublo 00 gauge model in the immediate post-war years. *Stephen Chapman archive*

BELOW: Approaching Liverpool from the south, Royal Scot class 4-6-0 No. 46134 *The Cheshire Regiment* passes Sefton Park with train 1K24 in around 1962. *Rev. David Benson*

ABOVE: The sprawling and impressive layout of running lines and sidings that was Edge Hill is shown to good effect in this panoramic view taken from Wavertree Road bridge on Friday 12th June 1959. Jubilee 4-6-0 No. 45695 *Minotaur* of Farnley Junction is approaching Liverpool with a Trans-Pennine express. On the left are the wagon shops and stretching away in the middle distance the vast marshalling yards known as the "Gridirons." Beyond the wagon shops is the Liverpool Corporation Passenger Transport tram and bus works while beyond the "Gridirons" and too far away to see clearly, is the Binns Road Meccano Ltd. factory. The railway in this view is much slimmed down now; the only sidings remaining are the nearest few beyond the four running lines, retained at the time of writing for staging wagons used on trains carrying imported biomass from the docks. *Stephen Chapman archive*

BELOW: Over at Liverpool Exchange, the erstwhile L&Y terminus, Hughes-Fowler "Crab" 2-6-0 No. 42942 awaits departure with the LCGB's Crab Commemorative Railtour to Goole on Saturday 8th October 1966. *Stephen Chapman archive*

ABOVE: The principal source of power for traffic on the L&Y lines in Liverpool, whether it be express passenger trains or the humblest dock and goods depot shunting duties, was Bank Hall engine shed - the site now occupied by Kirkdale electric train depot. This view inside the shed shows L&Y "Pug" 0F 0-4-0ST No. 51253 stored with one of the larger LMS Kitson 0F 0-4-0STs, some of which were built by BR. Behind them is Bank Hall's breakdown crane. *Stephen Chapman archive*

BELOW: In early BR days, Sunday 20th June 1948, ex-L&Y Class 6F 0-8-0 No. 12782 is pictured "on shed" still with its LMS number. It will soon become 52782. *Stephen Chapman archive*

ABOVE: Also at Bank Hall shed on 20th June 1948 is ex-L&Y 1F 0-6-0T No. 11535, to be 51535. The "Black Five" 4-6-0 on the right carries its interim BR number M4820 prior to becoming 44820. *Ben Brooksbank/Stephen Chapman archive*

BELOW: Southport retained a great deal of railway interest until comparatively recent times with vintage dc electrics until the 1980s, the Steamport Museum at the old engine shed, loco-hauled passenger trains and semaphore signalling. Here, in the 1950s or early '60s, an unidentified Stanier Class 3 2-6-2T removes empty coaches from the station. *Stephen Chapman archive*

ABOVE: With the motorman standing up to drive, a pair of 2-car Liverpool-Southport dc EMUs(later Class 502,) motor brake second No. M28354M leading, depart Southport in 1964 with a service to Crossens, on the Preston line. An intensive electric service ran between Southport and Crossens supplemented by Southport-Preston steam trains. Despite the services being used by two million passengers a year, they were withdrawn from 7th September and the line abandoned soon after. *Stephen Chapman archive*

BELOW: The venerable Pollitt Manchester, Sheffield & Lincolnshire Railway J10 0-6-0s were very much a feature of the Cheshire Lines Committee routes until some were sent to the Far East - Goole, for use on another joint line, the Axholme Joint. No. 65180 - a GC Robinson version J10/6 - is seen at the former CLC Walton shed at 11.10am on 3rd November 1956. *David Holmes*

ABOVE: When the present St. Helens Central station was known as Shaw Street, the then Central station (just St. Helens until 1949) was a terminus at the end of the Great Central Railway's branch from Lowton St. Mary's. It closed to passengers way back in March 1952 but freight continued until January 1965. This view on 21st September 1963 shows 4F 0-6-0 No. 44501 running round its train, the LCGB's South Lancashire Limited railtour which it has just brought from Horwich.

BELOW: Looking towards the end of the line, No. 44501 is seen to have run round and is ready to take the final leg of the tour back to Manchester Central. *Both Jack Wild/Stephen Chapman archive*

ABOVE: In the area immediately north of Earlestown station were Haydock Collieries and their railway system. Between 1869 and 1887 the Haydock company built six 0-6-0 well tanks at its own foundry, one of which, *Bellerophon*, has been preserved. This is 1874-built *Makerfield,* seen shunting at Haydock in 1951. *Stephen Chapman archive*

BELOW: And finally, at Liverpool's Edge Hill shed. On 26th March 1961 G2a 0-8-0 No. 49173, fresh out of works after overhaul, simmers in light steam while awaiting its next call to duty. No. 49173 is one of the Bowen-Cooke LNWR G1 class rebuilt from 1936 onwards with a G2 boiler and Belpaire firebox. Also visible on shed are "Jinty" 0-6-0T No. 47566, also ex-works, and 8P Pacific No. 46243 *City of Lancaster. Robert Anderson*

LANCASHIRE

RIGHT: The old cotton town of Bacup has no railway today but it was once the terminus of lines from Rochdale and Bury. Part of the latter now forms the East Lancashire Railway heritage line. The point of interest in this otherwise not great picture of Radial 2-4-2T No. 50652 in very early BR days is Bacup Shed signal box, whose name can best be described as down to earth. 'Twas ever thus in Bacup.

Bacup engine shed was situated well away from the station area on the Facit branch to Rochdale. This scene is dominated by the long-disused Height Barn Mill.
Stephen Chapman archive

ABOVE: Bacup's 4-road engine shed as seen on Sunday 15th March 1953. The engines present are Stanier 2-6-4 tanks Nos. 42619 and 42651. Bacup shed closed in 1954 but survived, derelict, into the 1960s.
Arthur Wilson

RIGHT: Bacup Station Ground Frame in December 1966, the time of closure.
Jack Wild/Stephen Chapman archive

ABOVE: Closure was still a good way off when this DMU was photographed at what looks to be a neat and tidy Bacup station following arrival from Manchester Victoria in March 1963. The DMU is one of the early non-standard Metro-Cammell sets with the yellow diamond coupling code.

BELOW: A Cravens DMU to Manchester Victoria awaits departure from Bacup on Saturday 3rd December 1966, the last day of services. Goods traffic had been withdrawn seven months earlier and as can be seen, the station sidings had already been lifted. The chimney belongs to the Plantation cotton mill. *Both Jack Wild/Stephen Chapman archive*

ABOVE: A busy last day moment at Bacup on 3rd December 1966. Alongside a Derby Works DMU is Stanier 2-6-4T No. 42644 on the LCGB's Rossendale Forrester railtour, a duty it shared with Ivatt Class 2 2-6-0 No. 46437. Behind the engine are the India cotton mill and the line into the closed goods yard. *Jack Wild/Stephen Chapman archive*

BELOW: Bacup and Todmorden are as if in two different worlds. Apart from Todmorden being in Yorkshire(not always the case as the town once straddled both counties,) a high ridge of wild moorland separates the two. This scene shows WD 2-8-0 No. 90548 blowing off steam while held in the loop at Hall Royd with Yorkshire-bound empties on Friday 25th March 1955 as a BR Standard Class 4 4-6-0 shunts the sidings. Through the murk in the left middle distance is the birthplace of Bellcode Books.
Stephen Chapman archive

ABOVE: On its way back to Lancashire, Brush Type 4 No. 47340 climbs past the former Robinwood Mill on the 1 in 65 up to Copy Pit summit with an engineers' spoil train from trackwork in the Todmorden area on 10th January 1988. *Stephen Chapman*

BELOW: Earby, between Colne and Skipton, was the junction for the branch to Barnoldswick. Pictured at Earby on Saturday 4th May 1963 is preserved LNER K4 2-6-0 No. 3442 *The Great Marquess* with the Railway Correspondence & Travel Society's Dalesman railtour from Bradford. *Jack Wild/Stephen Chapman archive*

ABOVE: The old lady on the level crossing at Barnoldswick seems unperturbed by the gricerly invasion following arrival of the RCTS Dalesman railtour on 4th May 1963. The swivel board signal is bound to be a point of considerable interest.

BELOW: Normality at Barnoldswick. It is Tuesday 7th May 1963 and school children - today's pensioners - head for home as parcels are unloaded from the Metro-Cammell DMU that has just arrived. The board signal is showing a different aspect to the picture above. Barnoldswick was closed to passengers from 27th September 1965 and completely in August 1966. Earby survived until February 1970 when the Skipton-Colne passenger service was withdrawn. *Both Jack Wild/Stephen Chapman archive*

ABOVE: Two of Accrington diesel depot's unique Cravens hydraulic transmission DMUs at Colne on Wednesday 23rd August 1967, the nearest with car No. M51747 leading on a Preston-Skipton service. These units were scrapped in the early 1970s as non-standard. Nowadays virtually all DMUs have hydraulic transmissions. Since 1970 Colne, which once boasted extensive sidings, goods yards and carriage sheds, has been a branch terminus, since reduced to a single platform at the end of a single line. *Stephen Chapman archive*

BELOW: A short distance along the line towards Rose Grove is Nelson station where Accrington shed's Stanier 2-6-4T No. 42437 is seen departing for Burnley and beyond in the 1950s. *Stephen Chapman archive*

ABOVE: In its day Rose Grove was an important junction where lines from Skipton, and Blackburn via Padiham met the Preston-Todmorden line; and there were extensive marshalling sidings and a motive power depot. This 1950s scene shows "Lanky" Radial Tank No. 50653 in the east-facing bay while on what appears to be a push-pull duty. Today, Rose Grove is still the junction between the branch from Colne and the line from Todmorden to Preston and the station is still open for business, but without its canopy while little else of the railway remains. *Stephen Chapman archive*

BELOW: The end is nigh. It is July 1968 and there are only a couple of weeks to go to the official end of British Rail standard gauge steam. Rose Grove was one of the last three steam depots on BR, the others also in Lancashire at Lostock Hall and Carnforth. Engines, mainly 8F 2-8-0s, sit on Rose Grove shed with little or no work to do. One of their last duties, if not the last on BR, was providing assistance to heavy trains climbing up to the summit of the Todmorden line at Copy Pit. Prominent in the picture is No. 48400.
Jack Wild/Stephen Chapman archive

ABOVE: More engines dumped unwanted at Rose Grove in July 1968. No. 48423 heads a trio of 8F 2-8-0s while next to it is "Black Five" 4-6-0 No. 45447.
Jack Wild/Stephen Chapman archive

LEFT: Drama at Accrington. The signalman at Accrington North box watches the spectacle as a "Black Five" 4-6-0 and a Hughes-Fowler "Crab" 2-6-0 turn off the line from Bury and blast their way eastwards towards the twisting viaduct some time during the 1960s.
Stephen Chapman archive

ABOVE: The scene at Blackburn station on 4th May 1963 when preserved LNER K4 2-6-0 No. 3442 *The Great Marquess* visited with the RCTS Dalesman railtour featured on page 72. Those were the days when railway enthusiasts really did wear anoraks - but then so did just about everyone else. *Jack Wild/Stephen Chapman archive*

BELOW: Like Bolton, Blackburn station displayed a model of an Isle of Man Steam Packet ferry until comparatively recent times. This is *Viking*, pictured on 10th January 1987. *Stephen Chapman*

ABOVE: The huge scale - and lost majesty - of Blackburn's twin trainsheds is apparent when set against a big locomotive such as preserved Merchant Navy Pacific No. 35028 *Clan Line,* seen calling there with a special to Carlisle on Saturday 11th May 1991. An air of dereliction pervades the whole station and at the turn of the century the trainshed was demolished - due in part to the state of the foundations supporting the trainshed walls - and replaced by a completely new station. *Both pictures on this page: Stephen Chapman*

BELOW: The station interior presents a fairly tidy image on 11th May 1991 with Pacer No. 142012 at the westbound face of the main island platform. Apart from the station buildings facing the street, the actual platforms are the only surviving part of the old station. The platform on the right, disused at the time of this shot, has been brought back into use but you would never recognise it.

ABOVE: West of Blackburn, Wakefield-allocated WD 2-8-0 No. 90412 thunders an unfitted express freight composed of empty coal wagons for Yorkshire through Cherry Tree station in March 1964. *Stephen Chapman archive*

BELOW: The diesel takeover is almost complete and "Black Five" 4-6-0 No. 45260 and a sister member of the class look hemmed in by the new order at Lostock Hall shed in July 1968. These diesels themselves have passed into history and as classics now attract as much enthusiast interest as steam. In this case they are a pair of the once ubiquitous BR/Sulzer Type 2s(Class 25,) with D5278 on the left. *Stephen Chapman*

ABOVE: With the end of steam only a week or two away, there's still work for 8F 2-8-0 No. 48723 on standby with the Lostock Hall tool vans. Despite the approaching end there were still several engines in steam here on this final Saturday of July 1968.

LEFT: One engine for whom the end did not mean the end. Though looking smart here, "Black Five" No. 45305 was sent to Hull for cutting up but while there she was rescued by the Humberside Locomotive Preservation Group and restored to full main line running order.
The Lostock Hall breakdown crane can be seen on the left.
Both Stephen Chapman

ABOVE: Diesels like Class 25 No. D5278 coming on shed have no need of Lostock Hall's giant coal hopper which is about to become redundant. Demolition of these strongly built edifices would be a challenge to any contractor brave enough to take on the job.

BELOW: Photography was strictly forbidden around the Ministry of Defence Royal Ordnance Factory at Chorley but while accompanying the daily Warrington-Blackburn freight in April 1992 the photographer managed to grab this shot of one of the depot's two 0-4-0 diesel hydraulic shunters in the BR exchange sidings. The pair were built by John Fowler & Co. of Leeds in 1962. This is *R.O.F. Chorley No. 3* **(builders' No. 4220021.)** *Malcolm Roughley/Stephen Chapman archive. Above: Stephen Chapman*

ABOVE: Tearing through Leyland with soutbound parcels train 3K17 on Saturday 17th August 1963 is rebuilt Patriot 4-6-0 No. 45512 *Bunsen* of Carlisle Upperby. *Stephen Chapman archive*

BELOW: Along the West Coast main line between Leyland and Preston is Farrington Junction where a curve to the Preston-Blackburn line turns off. In this 1965 scene "Black Five" 4-6-0 No. 45024 approaches from the south with a Down express.
Jack Wild/Stephen Chapman archive

ABOVE: On the same day as the previous photo, Britannia Pacific No. 70032 *Tennyson*, by this time lacking nameplates, blows off excess steam while working a southbound van train. The curve to the Blackburn line goes off to the right.
Jack Wild/Stephen Chapman archive

BELOW: The 3F 0-6-0T station pilot standing on the headshunt appears to attract the attention of the fireman on Jubilee 4-6-0 No. 45627 *Sierra Leone* as it rolls into Preston station from the south in the 1960s. *Arthur Chester*

ABOVE & BELOW: At the south end of Preston station in the early 1960s, Stanier Class 5 4-6-0 No. 45150 passes with a Down express freight(above) while Stanier Class 8P Pacific No. 46246 *City of Manchester* backs onto its train, The Lakes Express which it will take forward to Euston. In summer 1961 The Lakes Express was advertised as starting from Windermere at 11.5am(10.50 on Saturdays) with a portion from Workington Main and Keswick via Penrith. The Windermere train included a restaurant car. It was advertised to depart Preston at 12.48pm(12.43 on Saturdays,) reaching Euston nearly five hours later. The Down train left Euston at 11.35am.
Both Stephen Chapman archive

ABOVE: Summer Saturday passenger duty at Preston for a goods engine in the shape of ex-L&Y 3F 0-6-0 No. 52174 on 15th August 1953. There is no information as to the train but to an expert the tablet W546/1 on the smokebox door would no doubt reveal all. No. 52174 is carrying a 24D Lower Darwen shedplate and class A headlamps so it seems likely she has been pressed into service on a Blackpool-East Lancashire class A train - or else acting as a station pilot. The clock says 5.10pm while the raincoats, shiney platform on the right and general misty atmosphere suggest it is a typical drizzly summer's day. *Stephen Chapman archive*

BELOW: This veteran seen alive and well at home on Preston shed on Monday 17th April 1950 is sole surviving 1890-vintage ex-L&Y Class 2P 2-4-2T No. 46762. Prior to the 1923 Grouping, this engine had been on the Wirral Railway, having been sold by the L&Y. *Stephen Chapman archive*

ABOVE: Preston engine shed suffered a catastrophic fire in 1960 with part of the shed destroyed and several locomotives damaged. In this 1965 scene, the lofty spire of St. Walburge's church looks down on what little remains of the shed which is hosting a Metrovick Co-Bo diesel and a diesel shunter. A "Black Five" 4-6-0 simmers on the Blackpool line. *Both pictures: Jack Wild/Stephen Chapman archive*

BELOW: "Black Five" No. 44937 of Carlisle Upperby heads northbound out of Preston with a special working in August 1965.

ABOVE: On the same occasion as the previous photo, Farnley Junction's Jubilee 4-6-0 No. 45647 *Sturdee* crosses over to the Blackpool line with excursion 1X04 from West Yorkshire.

BELOW: Watched over by St. Walburge's, "Black Five" No. 45227 comes off the Blackpool line with an express to Euston on the same August 1965 day as the previous photos. *Both Jack Wild/Stephen Chapman archive*

ABOVE: And finally on that magical day in August 1965, the original Pacific named *Tornado* but with nameplates alas removed, BR Standard Britannia No. 70022, heads a pigeon special northbound out of Preston. *Jack Wild/Stephen Chapman archive*

BELOW: On Saturday 22nd September 1962, the RCTS Mid-Lancs Railtour ventured up the Preston & Longridge Joint line. The special, 1X23, is pictured here on arrival at the Longridge terminus under the charge of LMS-built G2a 0-8-0 No. 49451. On the right is the goods yard from where sidings once went to Cramp Oaks cotton mill. Although carrying both passengers(until 1930) and general goods(until 1967) the Longridge line primarily served Lord's and Tootle Height quarries further along the line from this view. It survived into the 1990s as far as Deepdale in Preston to serve a coal depot. *Arthur Wilson*

ABOVE: A timeless view looking towards Blackpool and the junction with the Fleetwood branch at Poulton le Fylde in 1991 - well not quite timeless, given the magnificent clock still adorning the platform. Much has changed since this view. The line has been totally modernized and electrified, the Fleetwood branch disconnected since the end of its freight traffic, the signal box eliminated and the station completely refurbished. *Stephen Chapman*

BELOW: At Fleetwood station in July 1963 with BR Standard Class 2 2-6-2T No. 84010, a locally-based engine, simmering at the platform. *Jack Wild/Stephen Chapman archive*

ABOVE: The photographer has turned slightly to his right to reveal this general view of Fleetwood station with a two-car Derby Works DMU present. The awning on the right edge of the trainshed covers the platform used by passengers for the Belfast and Isle of Man ferries which once sailed from a jetty on the far right. The Fleetwood terminus seen here closed to all traffic in April 1966, the line being shortened to Wyre Dock, the station there assuming the name Fleetwood until it too closed in June 1970.
Jack Wild/Stephen Chapman archive

BELOW: After the closure of Fleetwood, the branch remained in use serving Wyre power station until the early 1980s and until 1999 the adjoining Burn Naze ICI plant. A Class 47 is seen here at Hillylaid Crossing with tanks from Burn Naze to Stanlow in 1987. The Fleetwood branch is regarded as a strong candidate for reopening to passengers under the Government's "Restoring Your Railway" initiative announced in 2019 - if any of it ever happens! *Malcolm Roughley/Stephen Chapman archive*

ABOVE: At Kirkham Junction, the Preston-Blackpool line divided into three different routes to the resort. The most northerly was today's line to Blackpool North; in the centre, leaving via a flying junction, was the erstwhile line going direct to Blackpool Central, and on the south side today's line to Blackpool South which until 1964 also went to Central. This 1930s scene on the Blackpool South line shows an ex-Midland Railway 4F 0-6-0 passing Ansdell golf links while approaching Ansdell & Fairhaven station with a stopping service from Blackpool Central. *Ernest Sanderson/Stephen Chapman archive*

BELOW: The exterior of Blackpool Central station on Tuesday 6th October 1964. *Jack Wild/Stephen Chapman archive*

ABOVE: The Blackpool Central concourse on 6th October 1964. The station closed with effect from 2nd November and the railway was cut back to Blackpool South which is how it remains today.

BELOW: Still on 6th October 1964, the overcast weather, impending closure and a begrimed "Black Five" on coaching stock make a grim setting for this full extent view of Blackpool Central despite the magnificence of the famous tower.
All pictures on pages 92 and 93: Jack Wild/Stephen Chapman archive

ABOVE: Less tower, more train. A closer view of Blackpool Central and the "Black Five."

BELOW: Notable at Blackpool Central were the pair of old L&Y Barton Wright 0-4-4 tanks used as stationary boilers. By the time of this picture, again on 6th October 1964, they were in the process of being cut up, one reduced to just the frames and bunker.

LEFT: One can hardly visit Blackpool and ignore its trams. This view shows a vehicle less seen by the holidaying public - works car No. 3, pictured in Highfield Road during 1958.

CENTRE: Today Blackpool's everyday trams are the kind of modern light rail vehicles used by any urban network such as Manchester or Nottingham, maintained at a new purpose-built depot. But a heritage fleet has been kept for use at weekends and during the illuminations, and is still cared for at the original tram depot which until the 1960s had Central engine shed as a near neighbour.

Here we see a Standard tram in Hopton Road outside the depot in the 1960s. The florid number on the front defies identification but it looks like 28. In the background is Coliseum bus station. *Both Jack Wild/Stephen Chapman archive*

BOTTOM: The independent Knott End Railway ran from Garstang & Catterall station, on the West Coast main line north of Preston, to Garstang, Pilling and the coastal village of Knott End. It became part of the LMS in 1923 and BR in 1948. This is Garstang Town station looking east sometime after total closure in August 1965 - passenger services were withdrawn back in 1930 and the rest of the line to Pilling and Knott End closed in 1963 and 1950 respectively. On the left is the old island platform, on the right the goods shed. *S. Chapman archive*

ABOVE: Another minor branch from the West Coast main line to a coastal community was the LNWR line which left Lancaster Castle station and ran to Glasson Dock on the south bank of the Lune estuary. As well as the dock and Lancaster Quay it served a couple of factories, a small goods depot on Lune Road and an intermediate halt at Conder Green. The passenger service was withdrawn in July 1930 and freight to Glasson Dock ended in September 1964 but Lancaster Quay sidings continued until 1969. Stanier Class 5 2-6-0 No. 42952 is seen alongside Glasson Dock station(left) and the Lune estuary(right) with the Stephenson Locomotive Society's Northern Fells railtour of Sunday 29th May 1960. *Stephen Chapman archive*

BELOW: In 1906 the Midland Railway decided to go electric and it chose the Lancaster-Morecambe and Heysham route as its prototype, an electric service using a 25 cycles 6.6kv ac overhead system being introduced two years later. After a short spell of steam operation in the early 1950s, BR converted it to 50 cycles and installed new catenary, and this continued to operate until the line's closure in 1966. On Sunday 15th August 1965 with Driving Trailer Open Second No. M29021M leading, one of the four three-car electric units which operated the service enters Lancaster Green Ayre station while on a Lancaster Castle-Morecambe service. The grim fortifications of Lancaster Castle loom large in the background. *Stephen Chapman archive*

ABOVE: An unidentified Motor Open Brake Second heads a line of Lancaster, Morecambe & Heysham units lined up in the sidings at Morecambe Promenade on Sunday 29th May 1955. These are not the original Midland units but converted ex-LNWR Euston-Watford stock which were introduced at the time of the 1950s upgrade. *Stephen Chapman archive*

BELOW: Hest Bank was the ideal photographic location in pre-electrification days - one which could be combined with the annual summer holiday at Morecambe, especially before 1969 when the station closed to passengers. In this wonderful moment in time famous Stanier 8P Pacific No. 46220 *Coronation* skirts Morecambe Bay while heading a Glasgow-Birmingham express past Hest Bank on Thursday 24th August 1961. *Peter Cookson*

ABOVE: A little further north of Hest Bank is Bolton Le Sands where we see BR Standard Class 6 "Clan" Pacific No. 72001 *Clan Cameron* passing with a Glasgow-Liverpool express on Friday 27th April 1962. *Peter Cookson*

BELOW: Still at Bolton Le Sands, another interesting loco. The unique Royal Scot 4-6-0 No. 46170 *British Legion*, rebuilt in 1935 from the 1929-built experimental high pressure locomotive No. 6399 *Fury,* heads an Up express freight, also on Friday 27th April 1962. *Peter Cookson*

ABOVE: And then, just a little further north we reach Carnforth - the last bastion of BR standard gauge steam. Our arrival here on 4th July 1964 is greeted by the sight of pioneer BR Standard Pacific No. 70000 *Britannia* restarting the 11.50am Glasgow-Morecambe from a station stop. *Robert Anderson*

BELOW: By the Carnforth coaling plant on a Saturday towards the end of July 1968 is BR Standard Class 5 4-6-0 No. 73069. *Stephen Chapman*

ABOVE: Meanwhile, "Black Five" No. 45134 was having its fire cleaned - or maybe dropped for the last time - at the ash plant.

BELOW: Also in steam and still ready for work at Carnforth on this late July 1968 Saturday was "Black Five" No. 45017. Given that the end of standard gauge steam was only a week or so away, the working engines here were most creditably well groomed, at least on this particular day. *Both pictures on this page by Stephen Chapman*

ABOVE: Could the deployment of the less successful diesel classes to this part of the world have contributed to the relative longevity of steam here or were they deployed here because steam would be available to the end as standby for them? So far as these Clayton Type 1s were concerned, it was as much a case of the work for which they were intended drying up as anything else. Either way, the Furness lines had become something of a repository for less successful or non-standard types, adding to their already considerable interest. In this late July 1968 scene a pair of Claytons(later Class 17) stand in Carnforth Yard, No. D8513 the nearest.

BELOW: Also on shed was this Metropolitan Vickers Co-Bo diesel. These none too successful engines were banished to this part of the world in order to be near the Vickers works at Barrow where they could easily be repaired. The engine is displaying class 4 express freight discs which suggests it was still trusted with prestige workings - or was it just another case of a diesel instead of steam at any price. *Both Stephen Chapman*

RIGHT: Just inside the Carnforth shed doorway and proudly displaying the Carnforth 10A shedplate is now preserved BR Standard Class 4 4-6-0 No. 75027.
Stephen Chapman

BELOW: Willesden allocated Royal Scot No. 46126 *Royal Army Service Corps* had reached Carnforth on a running-in turn after a visit to Crewe Works. While there it was purloined for a Leeds job on 28th September 1962 and is seen here returning with the 1.53pm from Leeds.
Robert Anderson

ABOVE: Along the line from Carnforth to Settle Junction, "Black Five" No. 44758 has just passed over Wennington Junction and is approaching the station with the 8.5am Lancaster Green Ayre-Leeds stopping train on Saturday 27th July 1963. Here it will combine with the 8.5am Carnforth-Leeds whose coaches are already waiting in the bay platform at the east end of the station. *Peter Rose*

BELOW: Another one of those parts of Yorkshire which can be said to be in the North West. The last BR standard gauge steam locomotive to run on BR under its own power and one that is still running today - Britannia Pacific No. 70013 *Oliver Cromwell* - takes water at Hellifield while on the Warwickshire Railway Society's North Western Steam Tour of Saturday 18th May 1968. Starting at Coventry, it took in such places as Stockport, Todmorden, Preston, Blackburn and Morecambe. *Stephen Chapman archive*

CUMBRIA

ABOVE: A DMU delight. Some may question that but doubtless the arrival of the 12.42 Carlisle-Leeds at Dent was a delight for the passengers waiting on a wet Thursday 18th August 1988. Over the years the village of Dent has been in four different counties: Lancashire, Westmorland, Yorkshire, and nowadays Cumbria. *Stephen Chapman*

BELOW: "Black Five" No. 45148 of Carlisle Kingmoor rolls southbound through Ribblehead with a partly fitted express freight in 1965. *Jack Wild/Stephen Chapman archive*

ABOVE: Nearly there! On 1st April 1967 9F 2-10-0 No. 92009 makes a final push through a blizzard as it nears Ais Gill summit while on the Settle & Carlisle with a Long Meg-Widnes anhydrite train. *Robert Anderson*

BELOW: The market town of Kirkby Stephen was graced by two stations - the former Midland Railway West station on the Settle & Carlisle which remains open today, and East station on the former North Eastern Darlington-Penrith line via Stainmore, a fact which all readers will be acquainted with for sure. This is the engine shed at Kirby Stephen East on Sunday 25th May 1952. Even at this time the old NER 0-6-0s that worked the line had been largely replaced by more modern engines and those present here, are from left, Ivatt Class 2 2-6-0s Nos. 46478, 46476 and 46472. The tender of an NER 0-6-0 can be seen in the second shed doorway from left. Despite closure of the Stainmore line as long ago as 1962 the railway through here survived until 1974 to serve Hartley quarries which was long enough to enable the Stainmore Railway Company to eventually establish a railway heritage operation on the station site. *Arthur Wilson*

ABOVE: Deputising for a failed diesel, Heaton-allocated A3 Pacific No. 60083 *Sir Hugo* pulls The Waverley from Edinburgh to St. Pancras into a very chilly Appleby 31 minutes late on Boxing Day 1962. *Robert Anderson*

BELOW: On the much missed Cockermouth, Keswick and Penrith line, 2MT 2-6-0 No. 46432 calls at Keswick with a Workington-bound train on Monday 22nd May 1961. *Peter Rose*

ABOVE: Also on the CK & P line in 1961, one of the Derby Works lightweight diesel units that were among the very first in fleet service when introduced in the mid-1950s, calls at Bassenthwaite Lake while forming a Workington-Penrith service. *Stephen Chapman archive*

BELOW: With exactly one year to go to the official end of BR standard gauge steam, there was still plenty of action at Carlisle on Friday 11th August 1967. The scenario illustrated in the following five pictures began with 8F 2-8-0 No. 48111 arriving at Upperby sidings with a trip working conveying ballast from the quarries at Shap. A large collection of withdrawn locomotives, including several Class 2 2-6-0s, lies in store alongside Upperby carriage shed on the left. *Stephen Chapman*

ABOVE: The arrival of 48111 was followed by 9F 2-10-0 No. 92223 heading a northbound partly fitted express freight.

BELOW: Then came another Down express freight headed by a "Black Five" 4-6-0 believed to be 44819.
Both Stephen Chapman

ABOVE: No. 48111 awaits her next move at Upperby Sidings on 11th August 1967 while another steam loco shunts the yard in the right distance. On the left is the West Coast main line while right of 48111 are the lines which eventually lead to Bog Junction, the avoiding line and the Maryport line. Right of those is the curve leading round to connect with the Settle and Newcastle lines at London Road, all part of the complex layout of lines and connecting curves at Carlisle. On the far right can be seen the ash plant of Upperby motive power depot.
Stephen Chapman

LEFT: Semaphores (just about) and steam. A Britannia Pacific heads north for Kingmoor shed while 48111 goes about her business.
Stephen Chapman

ABOVE: On Tuesday 12th April 1955, antiquated looking ex-London & North Western "Cauliflower" 2F 0-6-0 No. 58412 basks in the sun outside the modern 1930s roundhouse at the former LNWR Upperby engine shed. *Stephen Chapman archive*

BELOW: On a less sunny day in the early 1950s, Royal Scot 4-6-0 No. 46148 *The Manchester Regiment* makes use of the turntable that formed the centrepiece of Upperby shed's American-style roundhouse. *Stephen Chapman archive*

ABOVE: Once again, outside Upperby shed, this time in the 1960s with 8P Pacific No. 46250 *City of Lichfield* in the sunshine. *Stephen Chapman archive*

BELOW: The mesmerizing tangle of lines and interconnecting curves to be found between Upperby and Carlisle station serve only to emphasize the importance of this major railway centre where the lines of six different pre-1923 railway companies converged. This early morning view from St. Nicholas Street bridge on 1st June 1963 shows on the far right a "Jinty" 3F 0-6-0T shunting coaches, then a Jubilee 4-6-0 is waiting to enter the station on the line from Durran Hill with an overnight Midland line express; Royal Scot 4-6-0 No. 46160 *Queen Victoria's Rifleman* heads south on the West Coast main line with the 6.15am stopping train to Crewe, and left, Ivatt Class 4 2-6-0 No. 43008 extends onto the Maryport line while shunting a parcels van. The bridge in the foreground carries lines into the goods station at Lancaster Street while those passing underneath lead to Bog Junction, the pair on the left being from Upperby and those on the right from the Midland line. From Bog Junction, lines continue to Currock Junction on the Maryport line, to Dentonholme North Junction forming an avoiding line for the station, and to Canal Junction connecting with the former North British lines. *Robert Anderson*

ABOVE: Another of the six engine sheds which Carlisle once boasted. This is the former Midland Railway shed at Durran Hill on the Settle line in July 1935 where Johnson 3F 0-6-0s Nos. 3311 and 3391 are seen in store. These engines are in original condition having not been rebuilt with Belpaire fireboxes and may well have already been withdrawn by this time. *Stephen Chapman archive*

BELOW: At Carlisle station on Saturday 19th August 1961, "Black Five" No. 45330 awaits departure with an Up express. *Stephen Chapman archive*

ABOVE: In this busy scene on 19th August 1961, BR Standard Class 6 Pacific No. 72009 *Clan Stewart* has arrived with an Up express which it will hand over to English Electric Type 4 No. D211 *Mauretania* seen waiting on the right. *Stephen Chapman archive*

BELOW: On the same day, Stanier Class 8P Pacific No. 46247 *City of Liverpool* stands ready with a good head of steam to take forward another southbound express. *Stephen Chapman archive*

ABOVE: Still on 19th August 1961, "Black Five" No. 44939 is also waiting to take over a southbound express. Behind it is an express hauled by a "Peak" Type 4 diesel which is likely to be bound for the Midland line to Leeds. *Both pictures: Stephen Chapman archive*

BELOW: Carlisle was one of those major junctions where east met west and ex-LNER engines rubbing shoulders with those from the LMS stable was the norm. In this 1960s view, A2 Pacific No. 60527 *Sun Chariot,* a Glasgow Polmadie engine by this time, is moving forward ready to take up the Scotland-bound express in the shadows on the right.

ABOVE: Even these doyens of the East Coast main line could occasionally be seen in normal service at Carlisle. A4 Pacific No. 60023 *Golden Eagle* is pictured on this occasion after replacing classmate No. 60004 *William Whitelaw* on the return leg of the RCTS Three Summit Railtour which ran from Leeds to Carstairs and Auchinleck and back on Sunday 30th June 1963.
Jack Wild/Stephen Chapman archive

BELOW: The former Caledonian Railway shed at Kingmoor, alive with smoke and steam in May 1965. "Black Five" No. 45236 is the one identifiable loco. *Jack Wild/Stephen Chapman archive*

ABOVE: Two of the four pre-Grouping engines preserved in working order by BR's Scottish Region took part in the RCTS Solway Ranger railtour of Saturday 13th June 1964 which ran from Leeds to Carlisle and took in various Cumbrian branches. Caledonian Railway single No.123 and Great North of Scotland 4-4-0 No. 49 *Gordon Highlander* worked the train between Carlisle and Silloth where No. 123 is pictured. *Stephen Chapman archive*

BELOW: Great North of Scotland 4-4-0 No. 49 *Gordon Highlander* (BR Class D40 No. 62277) makes use of the old turntable at Silloth while involved with the RCTS Solway Ranger railtour of 13th June 1964. Silloth closed to all traffic just three months later, the closure effective from 7th September. *Stephen Chapman archive*

ABOVE: The Calva & Linefoot branch of the Cleator & Workington Junction Railway ran from Calva Junction, Workington, and, serving Buckhill Colliery on the way, connected at Linefoot with a branch from Brigham, on the CK & P, to Bullgill on the Maryport & Carlisle. It had closed north of Buckhill Colliery by the 1930s but the remaining section survived until the end of the Cold War to serve the high security NATO munitions depot at Broughton Moor. This rare view on the Buckhill branch in 1985 shows Class 47 No. 47206 heading a military stores train out on weed covered track at the remains of Seaton station which had closed to passengers as long ago as 1922. *Malcolm Roughley*

BELOW: Still on the Cleator & Workington Junction Railway, at Workington Central station where ex-Furness Railway 3F 0-6-0 No. 52501, rebuilt with a Lancashire & Yorkshire Aspinall pattern boiler, is on the Stephenson Locomotive Society's West Cumberland railtour of Sunday 5th September 1954. *Neville Stead collection/Transport Library*

ABOVE: On shed at Workington Main on Wednesday 1st September 1954 is No. 52494, a Furness Railway 0-6-0 with the original large boiler. Designed by W. F. Pettigrew, these engines dated from 1913. This one was unusual in that it had been rebuilt with an L&Y boiler but at some point had reverted to an original Furness boiler. *Neville Stead collection/Transport Library*

BELOW: Ex-LNWR "Cauliflower" 0-6-0 No. 58412 pictured at Workington Main shed(according to information that came with the negative) in the early 1950s. These engines were a feature of the line to Keswick and Penrith until replaced by the Ivatt Class 2 2-6-0s. *H.C. Casserley/Stephen Chapman archive*

ABOVE: An interesting scene at Whitehaven Bransty on 15th March 1955. Ex-Furness Railway 3F 0-6-0 No. 52499 moves empty coaching stock northbound away from the station and past William Colliery. The line of NCB wagons adds further interest.
E.E. Smith/Neville Stead collection/Transport Library

BELOW: The surface buildings, equipment and railway for Haigh and Ladysmith collieries which extended far out under the Irish Sea, were situated high up on the cliff tops overlooking Whitehaven from the south. Their railways were connected by inclines down to both the harbour and to the BR main line at Corkickle. Giesel ejector-fitted Barclay 0-4-0ST *King* (built 1919, builder's No. 1448) is seen here shunting at Ladysmith on Monday 14th August 1972. *Adrian Booth.*

ABOVE: This rare shot shows a Class 40 propelling loaded wagons along the short branch to the low level nuclear waste disposal point at Drigg while working the daily Carlisle-Barrow class 8 trip in 1974. The load has come from the Sellafield reprocessing plant which can be seen making its presence known above the dunes. *Malcolm Roughley*

BELOW: Given the bountiful supply of high grade iron ore and coking coal in Furness and West Cumbria it's no surprise that several large iron and steel plants grew up along the coast. This undated but probably early 1950s scene shows Barrow steelworks No.5, an ex-Furness Railway Sharp Stewart 0-4-0ST. *H. C. Casserley/Stephen Chapman archive*

ABOVE: Shipyard cranes overlook the scene at Buccleuch Dock sidings, Barrow, on Tuesday 22nd June 1965 where Hudswell Clarke 204hp 0-6-0 diesel mechanical 0-6-0 shunter No. D2516 is on duty. Seven of these engines, which were similar to those seen on the Manchester Ship Canal Railway on page 45, were allocated to Barrow for shunting. They were among the many types of shunters withdrawn as non-standard in the late 1960s. *Stephen Chapman archive*

BELOW: An unidentified Class 25 prepares to leave Barrow Yard with a class 7 freight for Carnforth in 1974. Cavendish Dock is on the left. *Malcolm Roughley*

ABOVE: Plumpton Junction is best known as the point where the Lakeside branch, today's Lakeside & Haverthwaite Railway, left the Barrow-Carnforth main line. But there was another branch going the opposite way, the Bardsea branch to Conishead Priory on the north shore of Morecambe Bay. On the way it crossed the Ulverston Canal and served North Lonsdale iron and steel works, the site of which became the Glaxo pharmaceutical plant. At Plumpton Junction in 1991, Glaxo's own Class 08 shunter *Ulverstonian*(08678) prepares to set off along the short branch back to the Glaxo works with incoming tank wagons. On the right a triangle of industrial lines once went to Plumpton quarries. Glaxo also had a Barclay 0-4-0 fireless steam locomotive(2268 of 1949) which in 1991 was the last steam locomotive of any kind to see commercial use in Britain, leaving for preservation later in 1992. *Malcolm Roughley*

BELOW: In 1974 a Class 40 heads a Barrow-bound train of hopper wagons through Grange over Sands. *Malcolm Roughley*

ABOVE: Back to steam days. Fowler Class 4 2-6-4T No. 42369 makes a stirring start out of Oxenholme with a local service to Windermere at 3.32pm on Saturday 21st April 1962. *Peter Cookson*

BELOW: In 1966, "Black Five" No. 44675 ambles light engine through Kendal station. The phenomenal amount of parcels traffic just about fills the entire platform. In all liklihood it consists of countless pairs of K shoes which were made in Kendal until 2003. Any amount of parcels traffic on stations is now a thing of the past. *Stephen Chapman archive*

ABOVE: A great railway show not generally available to the public - at least not from the lineside - was the sight of a steam locomotive picking up water at speed from the water troughs. "Black Five" No. 45105 kicks up a powerful spray while topping up from Dillicar Troughs as it heads a Morecambe-Glasgow relief on 31st July 1965 - soaking the photographer in the process. *Robert Anderson*

BELOW: In this Dillicar Troughs scene on Saturday 22nd August 1964, the driver of Jubilee 4-6-0 No. 45554 *Ontario* on the 8.50am Blackpool-Glasgow has indicated that he is not confident in his engine's ability to make it unaided over Grayrigg and Shap summits, and so a pilot in the shape of Tebay's Fowler 2-6-4T No. 42414 - probably out-based at Oxenholme since closure of the shed there - is providing front end assistance. No. 42414 was withdrawn only a couple of months after this event. *Robert Anderson*

ABOVE: With the aid of a 2-6-2T from Tebay on the rear, an 8F 2-8-0 slogs up the 1 in 75 to Shap Summit in the early 1950s.

BELOW: As the rear of the above train finally passes the identity of the banking engine is revealed as Fowler Class 3 2-6-2T No. 40070.
Both Tom Greaves

ABOVE: A view which like no other illustrates the disfigured front end of a Duchess Pacific after removal of the streamlined casing. This one is No. 46225 *Duchess of Gloucester* appearing to make light work of an early 1950s northbound express while climbing unassisted up to Shap.

BELOW: An unrebuilt Royal Scot which appears to be 46156 *The South Wales Borderer* climbs Shap as Ivatt Class 8P Pacific No. 46257 *City of Salford* descends the other way. *Both Tom Greaves*

ABOVE: An unidentified Compound Class 4P 4-4-0 provides front end assistance to a "Black Five" near Scout Green in the early 1950s *Tom Greaves*

BELOW: Also heading an express near Scout Green in the early 1950s is Newton Heath Jubilee 4-6-0 No. 45710 *Irresistible*, **one of those with a Fowler small tender.** *Tom Greaves*

ABOVE: This time it's Princess Royal Pacific No. 46208 *Princess Helena Victoria* heading by with a 1950s express. *Tom Greaves*

BELOW: In this 1950s scene "Black Five" 4-6-0 No. 45248 pilots a Jubilee 4-6-0 on an Up express. *Tom Greaves*

ABOVE: The brutalist look of ex-Crosti-boilered 9F 2-10-0 No. 92025 presents a forceful impression as it thunders over Scout Green level crossing with a heavy northbound freight in 1967. *Stephen Chapman archive*

BELOW: It's 8.35 in the morning on 27th July 1963 and ex-Midland Railway 4F 0-6-0 No. 43908 is shunting the yard at Penrith while on pick-up goods duty. *Robert Anderson*